Music
Through Time

CLARINET BOOK 2

SELECTED AND
EDITED BY

Paul Harris

MUSIC DEPARTMENT

OXFORD

UNIVERSITY PRESS

OXFORD
UNIVERSITY PRESS

Great Clarendon Street, Oxford OX2 6DP, England
198 Madison Avenue, New York, NY 10016, USA

Oxford University Press is a department of the University of Oxford.
It furthers the University's aim of excellence in research, scholarship,
and education by publishing worldwide

14th impression, 2014

ISBN 978 0 19 357185 3

Printed in Great Britain

All of the pieces in this collection are arranged
for clarinet and piano by Paul Harris

CONTENTS

16th century
Danse Française

This was an era of great change. For Europeans, new worlds were discovered. The Renaissance had a big effect on the arts and the Reformation challenged the ideas of the Catholic Church. In the East, the Persian Empire grew to rival that of the Ottoman Turks who had advanced into central Europe as far as Hungary. In India, the great Moghul Empire was in control.

Claude Gervaise
(*fl.* 16th century)

Gervaise was a composer and viol player. Among his many compositions were six books of dances; this piece is taken from one of them.

1689
Lilliburlero

The French king Louis XIV, the Sun King, declared war on England. In Russia, Tsar Peter the Great seized power, forcing his half-sister to retire to a convent. Aphra Behn, England's first professional woman writer, was honoured by being buried in Westminster Abbey.

Henry Purcell
(1659–95)

The origin of this tune is unknown. It appeared in Purcell's *Musick's Handmaid* as 'A New Irish Tune', and more recently has been used as a nursery rhyme and a radio signature tune.

The Freemasons were established—a secret society with elaborate rituals and a handshake that only fellow members could recognize. The Golden Lion became the first coffee house in London to admit women. School attendance became compulsory in Prussia.

Handel provided this music for a royal water party in honour of King George I. It took place on the River Thames in July and his suite is known today as the 'Water Music'.

Trio

George Frideric Handel
(1685–1759)

The great patron of the arts, Frederick of Prussia, died. His state, which had all but doubled in size, was feared throughout Europe. This enlightened despot liked wearing a tunic full of bullet-holes and rarely, if ever, visited his wife, Elizabeth of Brunswick.

This andante is taken from a set of pieces for two basset horns. Mozart also used this member of the clarinet family in his last opera, *The Magic Flute*, and in his Requiem.

1786
Andante

Wolfgang Amadeus Mozart
(1756–91)

1802
Melody

Jean Xavier Lefèvre
(1763–1829)

While writing his second symphony, Beethoven noticed the onset of his deafness. His hearing subsequently deteriorated until he became totally deaf some 17 years later. John Dalton introduced his atomic theory, which ultimately proved to be the foundation of modern chemistry.

Lefèvre was an important figure in the history of the clarinet. He wrote an important tutor which contains the first known sonatas for the instrument.

1810
Écossaise

Ludwig van Beethoven
(1770–1827)

The Chinese 'Dragon Lady', Zheng Yi Sao, who led a pirate fleet of 1,800 junks and 70,000 men and women, surrendered to the Governor-General, Bai Ling. She was evidently a very successful negotiator, as none of the pirates were punished and she joined the Chinese navy!

Beethoven is well known as a composer of full-scale symphonies but he also wrote short, tuneful pieces like this *Écossaise*.

OXFORD

Music Through Time

CLARINET BOOK 2
PIANO ACCOMPANIMENTS

CONTENTS

SELECTED AND EDITED BY
Paul Harris

16th century
Danse Française

This was an era of great change. For Europeans, new worlds were discovered. The Renaissance had a big effect on the arts and the Reformation challenged the ideas of the Catholic Church. In the East, the Persian Empire grew to rival that of the Ottoman Turks who had advanced into central Europe as far as Hungary. In India, the great Moghul Empire was in control.

Claude Gervaise
(*fl.* 16th century)

Gervaise was a composer and viol player. Among his many compositions were six books of dances; this piece is taken from one of them.

The French king Louis XIV, the Sun King, declared war on England. In Russia, Tsar Peter the Great seized power, forcing his half-sister to retire to a convent. Aphra Behn, England's first professional woman writer, was honoured by being buried in Westminster Abbey.

The origin of this tune is unknown. It appeared in Purcell's *Musick's Handmaid* as 'A New Irish Tune', and more recently has been used as a nursery rhyme and a radio signature tune.

Lilliburlero

Henry Purcell
(1659–95)

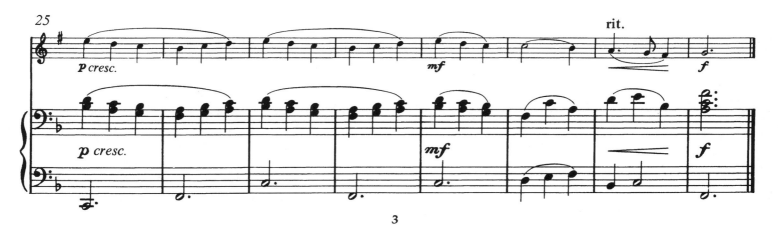

1717
Trio

George Frideric Handel
(1685–1759)

The Freemasons were established—a secret society with elaborate rituals and a handshake that only fellow members could recognize. The Golden Lion became the first coffee house in London to admit women. School attendance became compulsory in Prussia.

Handel provided this music for a royal water party in honour of King George I. It took place on the River Thames in July and his suite is known today as the 'Water Music'.

4

D.C. al Fine

1786
Andante

Wolfgang Amadeus Mozart
(1756–91)

The great patron of the arts, Frederick of Prussia, died. His state, which had all but doubled in size, was feared throughout Europe. This enlightened despot liked wearing a tunic full of bullet-holes and rarely, if ever, visited his wife, Elizabeth of Brunswick.

This andante is taken from a set of pieces for two basset horns. Mozart also used this member of the clarinet family in his last opera, *The Magic Flute*, and in his Requiem.

While writing his second symphony, Beethoven noticed the onset of his deafness. His hearing subsequently deteriorated until he became totally deaf some 17 years later. John Dalton introduced his atomic theory, which ultimately proved to be the foundation of modern chemistry.

Lefèvre was an important figure in the history of the clarinet. He wrote an important tutor which contains the first known sonatas for the instrument.

Jean Xavier Lefêvre
(1763–1829)

1810
Écossaise

Ludwig van Beethoven
(1770–1827)

The Chinese 'Dragon Lady', Zheng Yi Sao, who led a pirate fleet of 1,800 junks and 70,000 men and women, surrendered to the Governor-General, Bai Ling. She was evidently a very successful negotiator, as none of the pirates were punished and she joined the Chinese navy!

Beethoven is well known as a composer of full-scale symphonies but he also wrote short, tuneful pieces like this *Écossaise*.

Napoleon died in exile on the island of St Helena in the South Atlantic,
far from the European battleground he had ruled with mastery.
Michael Faraday invented the electric motor.

In 1935 an American newspaper carried the following report: 'At
Lawton, Oklahoma, John Brett, an attorney, sang *Home, Sweet Home*
to a jury so as to induce clemency for his client, a bank robber. The
jury responded with a verdict of life imprisonment.'

Home, Sweet Home

Sir Henry Bishop
(1786–1855)

1826
Who is Sylvia?

The Royal Zoological Society was founded. It took over the existing menagerie at the Tower of London, and opened the London Zoo two years later. The first railway tunnel opened, on the Liverpool–Manchester line.

Many composers have made musical settings of this text from Shakespeare's *The Two Gentlemen of Verona*. Schubert's is one of more than 600 songs he wrote during his brief life.

Franz Schubert
(1797–1828)

1848
Melody

Giuseppe Concone
(1801–61)

The first ever convention on women's rights in the USA was organized by the anti-slavery campaigners Lucretia Mott and Elizabeth Stanton. They demanded the right to vote and equality under the law in education, marriage, and work. Amelia Jenks Bloomer designed a 'practical and respectable' undergarment which was named after her.

Concone was a respected Italian teacher and composer of songs and singing exercises.

Andante con moto

1878
The Barrel Organ

Pyotr Ilyich Tchaikovsky
(1840–93)

The obelisk known as 'Cleopatra's Needle' arrived in London, over 3,300 years after it was first erected in Ancient Egypt. The painter James Whistler won damages of a farthing in a libel case against a rude critic! The CID (Criminal Investigation Department) was set up at New Scotland Yard in London.

The barrel organ was a mechanical organ operated by turning a handle. It was restricted to a number of predetermined tunes, like a musical box.

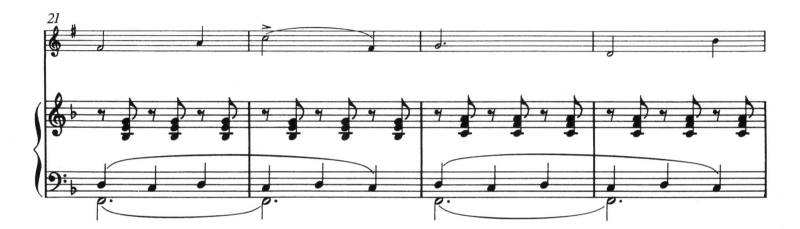

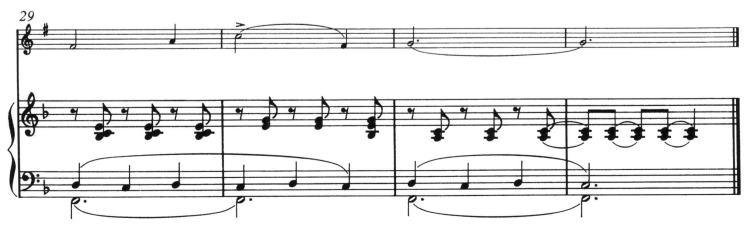

1892
Old Man's Tale

Enrique Granados
(1867–1916)

Colourful posters by Toulouse-Lautrec appeared in Paris advertising the cabaret at the Moulin Rouge. The fashion magazine *Vogue* first appeared in New York—England had to wait 24 years for the English edition. The exuberant American poet Walt Whitman died.

Granados was a Spanish composer and virtuoso pianist. He and his wife were tragically killed when the liner they were travelling on was torpedoed by a German U-boat during World War I.

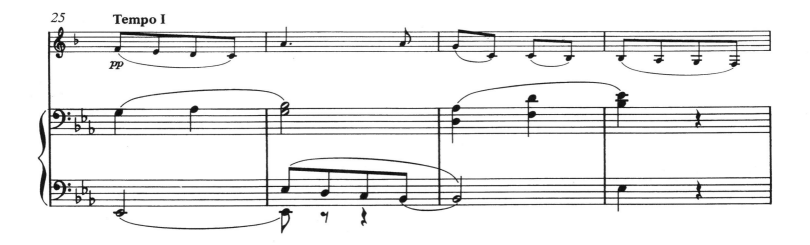

1911
When your hair is like the snow

Scott Joplin

(1868–1917)

The motorized washing-machine was invented in the USA. The physicist Ernest Rutherford showed that the atom had a structure like a miniature solar system. The General Strike brought Britain to a standstill.

Among the most well-known pieces by Scott Joplin are the *Maple Leaf Rag*, and *The Entertainer*, the latter popularized by its use in the film *The Sting*.

The tomb of Tutankhamun was discovered by the archaeologist Howard Carter. The Fascist movement, led by Mussolini, seized power in Italy. BBC radio went on the air.

Janáček was very influenced by Moravian folk-music and carried a sketch-book with him so that he could write down any interesting new melodies he heard.

1922
Two Moravian Folk-songs
Leos Janáček
(1854–1928)

I. Andante

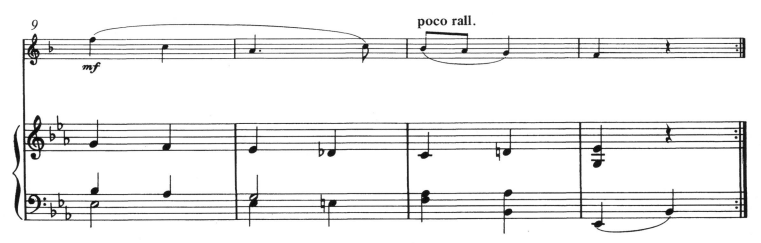

II. Allegretto

Stalin's rival, Leon Trotsky, was assassinated with an ice-pick in Mexico City. Disney Pictures released the cartoon film *Fantasia*, still popular today. Many Jewish artists, composers, and scientists fled from Europe to America to escape the Nazi regime. Duke Ellington became well-known in the USA.

Walton wrote many film scores including *The Battle of Britain*, *The First of the Few*, and *Henry V*.

1940
Song at Dusk

William Walton
(1902–83)

1990
Chalumeau Sonatina

Paul Harris
(1957–)

The Chalumeau was an early version of today's clarinet. Nowadays we use the term to refer to the lovely low register of the instrument. This three-movement Sonatina makes full use of its dark, brooding qualities in the slow middle movement.

I

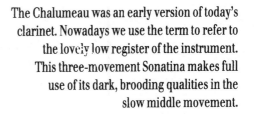

II

Lento espressivo

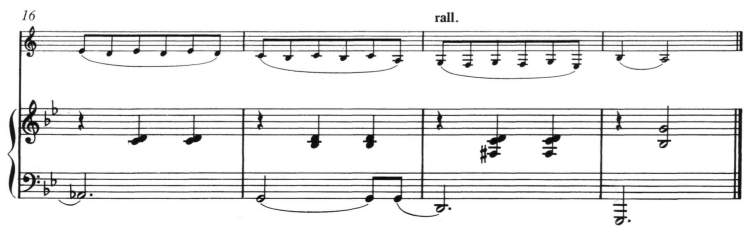

III

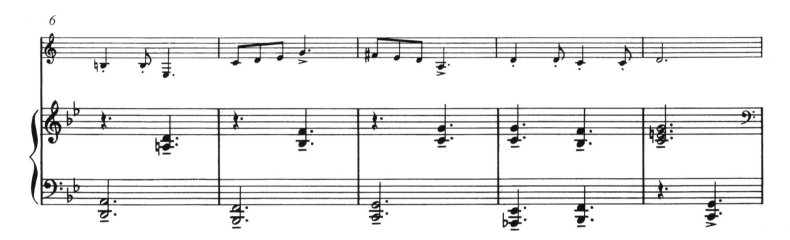

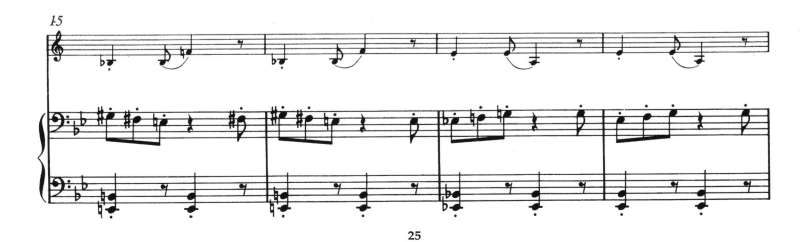

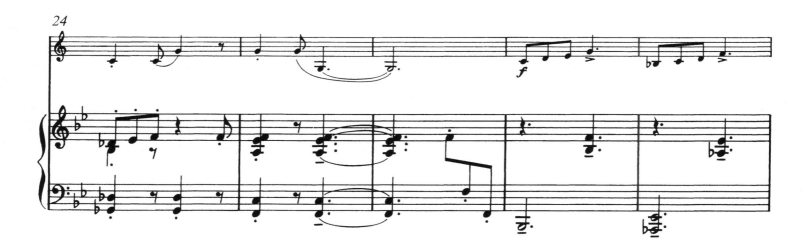

Napoleon died in exile on the island of St Helena in the South Atlantic, far from the European battleground he had ruled with mastery. Michael Faraday invented the electric motor.

In 1935 an American newspaper carried the following report: 'At Lawton, Oklahoma, John Brett, an attorney, sang *Home, Sweet Home* to a jury so as to induce clemency for his client, a bank robber. The jury responded with a verdict of life imprisonment.'

1821
Home, Sweet Home

Sir Henry Bishop
(1786–1855)

The Royal Zoological Society was founded. It took over the existing menagerie at the Tower of London, and opened the London Zoo two years later. The first railway tunnel opened, on the Liverpool–Manchester line.

Many composers have made musical settings of this text from Shakespeare's *The Two Gentlemen of Verona*. Schubert's is one of more than 600 songs he wrote during his brief life.

1826
Who is Sylvia?

Franz Schubert
(1797–1828)

1848
Melody

Giuseppe Concone
(1801–61)

The first ever convention on women's rights in the USA was organized by the anti-slavery campaigners Lucretia Mott and Elizabeth Stanton. They demanded the right to vote and equality under the law in education, marriage, and work. Amelia Jenks Bloomer designed a 'practical and respectable' undergarment which was named after her.

Concone was a respected Italian teacher and composer of songs and singing exercises.

1878
The Barrel Organ

Pyotr Ilyich Tchaikovsky
(1840–93)

The obelisk known as 'Cleopatra's Needle' arrived in London, over 3,300 years after it was first erected in Ancient Egypt. The painter James Whistler won damages of a farthing in a libel case against a rude critic! The CID (Criminal Investigation Department) was set up at New Scotland Yard in London.

The barrel organ was a mechanical organ operated by turning a handle. It was restricted to a number of predetermined tunes, like a musical box.

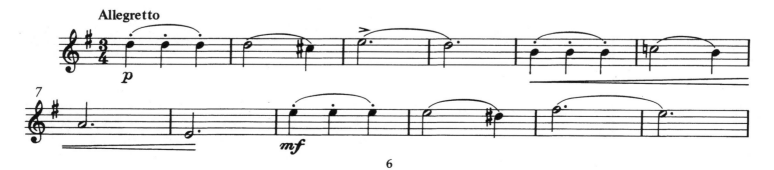

Colourful posters by Toulouse-Lautrec appeared in Paris advertising the cabaret at the Moulin Rouge. The fashion magazine *Vogue* first appeared in New York—England had to wait 24 years for the English edition. The exuberant American poet Walt Whitman died.

Granados was a Spanish composer and virtuoso pianist. He and his wife were tragically killed when the liner they were travelling on was torpedoed by a German U-boat during World War I.

1892
Old Man's Tale

Enrique Granados
(1867–1916)

1911
When your hair is like the snow
Scott Joplin
(1868–1917)

The motorized washing-machine was invented in the USA. The physicist Ernest Rutherford showed that the atom had a structure like a miniature solar system. The General Strike brought Britain to a standstill.

Among the most well-known pieces by Scott Joplin are the *Maple Leaf Rag*, and *The Entertainer*, the latter popularized by its use in the film *The Sting*.

1922
Two Moravian Folk-songs*
Leos Janáček
(1854–1928)

The tomb of Tutankhamun was discovered by the archaeologist Howard Carter. The Fascist movement, led by Mussolini, seized power in Italy. BBC radio went on the air.

Janáček was very influenced by Moravian folk-music and carried a sketch-book with him so that he could write down any interesting new melodies he heard.

I. Andante

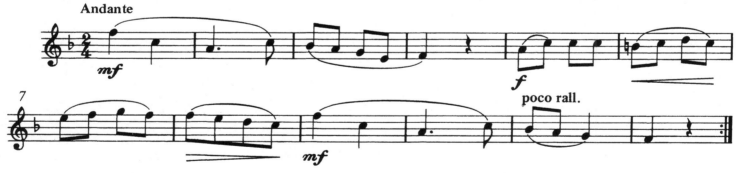

II. Allegretto

Stalin's rival, Leon Trotsky, was assassinated with an ice-pick in Mexico City. Disney Pictures released the cartoon film *Fantasia*, still popular today. Many Jewish artists, composers, and scientists fled from Europe to America to escape the Nazi regime. Duke Ellington became well-known in the USA.

Walton wrote many film scores including *The Battle of Britain*, *The First of the Few*, and *Henry V*.

1940
Song at Dusk

William Walton
(1902–83)

The Chalumeau was an early version of today's clarinet. Nowadays we use the term to refer to the lovely low register of the instrument. This three-movement Sonatina makes full use of its dark, brooding qualities in the slow middle movement.

1990
Chalumeau Sonatina

Paul Harris
(1957–)

I

II

III